MW01231051

ELEPHANT

An Animal with

Mystical Features

Dedicated to My Family

GEORGE MALIAKAL

This Book edition is published in 2019 by
GLAN BOOKS
21 Uma Nagar, Thrissur 680655, Kerala, India.

Copyright (c): Maj. George Maliakal (Retd.)
E-mail ID: gcmaliakal@221045@gmail.com

All rights reserved

Publishers   and the Author acknowledge with thanks for the invaluable information that is available on the Internet. This information is gathered , processed, grouped and presented in this book for creating awareness among he people on the subject across the world.. We also acknowledge with thanks and state that some of the pictures included in this book are from the Internet and they are owned by the respective owners of their websites.

ISBN:
Price:

Contents

The Biggest Silver Coin issued with Elephant's Picture.
The Coin is 650 mm diameter , weighs 55 Kgs and
made from .999 pure silver.

Preface

This book titled " Elephant - An Animal with Mystical Features " is very special to me; because it has something very unique about it, its theme, its presentation and the circumstances, which made me to create this book. I never had thought of creating a book like this.

It is the innovative thought that came to me while participating in the recently held Coin Exhibition 'Mudra 2019' at our home city Thrissur, that inspired me to create this wonderful book on 'Elephant'.

Initially, I was totally blank about this project. Main source of my information was Internet, the 'Online World', other reading materials and discussion with elephant owners and elephant lovers.

I started exploring the Online World and I got everything I was looking for. I knew, it would be a very difficult task for me, to create something like this, to gather all the information, study them, group them into various topics, and make them in a readable content with pictures, and present it to the world.

Here I would like to mention that I have tried my best to gather maximum information on elephants, and share with you all the relevant information and facts that you, the world need to know. Please read through the content, understand the present challenges elephants are facing across the world . Now, it is for you to decide whether you would like to take some action or not.

I am glad, I could complete this book fully to my satisfaction. If I you like my book, pl mark it as your favourite collections and share it with your family and friends. I would also appreciate your reviews/ comments on my book. Thank you.

George Maliakal
Author

Elephant herd enjoying their habitat life.

Elephant herd enjoying their habitat life.

The senior female of the herd along with other elephants mourn near the dead body of one the members of their group.

1
Interesting Facts about Elephant

Elephants are also very fascinating creatures with funny habits. So why not spend some time learning them new things about the big fellows?

Not only is the elephant a very intelligent creature, it's also an animal of mystery with loads of secrets yet to be uncovered. Did you know that they need sun cream just as much as we do?

Elephant - The Majestic Animal
Nothing can be compared the majestic buildup of an elephant and when you ride on when, it feels like you've gone back to the times of the royal. It is a fact that elephant has a beautiful majestic look. But often we get scared when we encounter an elephant or a herd (elephants in groups) very close because it could do anything, especially when their trainer is not with them.

Elephants are some of the most intelligent animals on Earth.

Communication is vital to elephants, who rely on a social network for survival. Although elephants can make a very wide range of sounds (10 octaves), they mostly communicate through low-frequency sounds called "rumbling." In fact, elephanElephants are some of the most intelligent animals on Earth.ts are capable of producing and perceiving sounds one to two octaves lower than the human hearing limit. A greeting is also in place and whenever they meet another one from their family; they will greet them with a quiet rumbling sound.

Elephant with Mystical Features: The physical characteristics, size, shape and its intelligence which make this animal, elephant as the most liked, useful, wanted and appreciated animal in this world. And due to its physical characteristics, life style and, this animal can only survive in certain parts of the world. And I have already explained above, it is due to this consideration, everyone, whether, an individual, family, organization/ country, all would like to have this biggest and beautiful and very intelligent animal in their country. This might surprise many.

Elephants Role in the Ecosystem: Elephants, play an important role in maintaining the biodiversity of the ecosystems in which they live. They flatten forests and dense grasslands, creating habitat for smaller species. African elephants also dig water holes, which are also used by other species.

Elephants helps in generating Green growth. Elephants travel long distances in search for food, dispersing seeds contained in their waste along the way. This helps to generate new green growth. In some areas, species of plants and trees rely entirely upon elephants for seed dispersal for their survival.

Social life. Elephant families are led by female Elephants, the elephant's social structure is quite different to other animals. The female elephants live in a family unit, also called a herd, of up to 25 elephants with a female elephant in the lead. There is a clear hierarchy usually based on age and experience, so the older the elephant is, the stronger their influence is in the herd.

Male elephants, however, usually leave their family between the age of eight and 15. In other words, when they have become real teenage elephants. After this they wander around in small temporary herds whilst they search for females willing to make new "elephant babies. "hey don't need much sleep

Sleep: While human beings require (on average) eight hours sleep for total functionality, elephants are way more flexible. They only sleep four hours per night and they even spend half of their sleep standing up. Deep sleep, however, requires a bit more effort and the elephant would usually lay on its side whilst snoring out loudly. Not so different from you and me, are they?

Elephants and temple festivals: Even though elephants can live for 60 years, they often die way before as a result of injury or decease.

Elephants get emotional when they experience someone dying. They turn silent and take time to mourn the dead elephant, and sometimes they even cover dead relatives with grass or soil. It is also proven that the big animals are quite scared of ants and bees, which reveal that despite their big size, elephants are gentle.

Elephants are highly social animals with incredible memories. This could be attributed to their large brains, which can reach over 5kg in mass!

Elephants not only have huge bodies, they also have a brain that weights five kilograms, so it's no surprise that they are very intelligent animals. With their large size and brain capacity, they can store information and remember things for years, not just skills necessary for their survival but social learning as well. Elephants remember other individuals and are able to recognize them when they meet them again, even several years later!

Their memory is impressive. This high memory power make them very superior among other animals. Elephants really do have long and sharp memory.

Elephants have an extremely slow pulse rate, around 27 beats per minute. Compare that to the average human (80 bpm), or Canary (1000 bpm).

Elephants can give birth until they're 50 and an Elephant's life expectancy is 60- 70 years old. The oldest on record– an Asian Elephant named Lin Wang– died at the ripe old age of 86.

There are three distinct species of elephant left in the world: The Asian elephant and Africa has the forest and savannah elephant species.

The word "elephant" comes from the Greek word *"elephas"* which means ivory".

The elephant's gestation period is 22 months – longer than any other land animal in the world. A new born human baby weighs an average of 7 pounds while a new born elephant baby can weigh up to 260 pounds! The baby can stand up shortly after being born.

The oldest known elephant in the world lived for 86 years (1917 – 2003). The average lifespan of an elephant is from 50 to 70 years. The largest known elephant was shot in Angola in 1956 and weighed about 24 000 pounds! It had a shoulder height of 3.96 metres!

The tusks of an elephant are modified incisors that grow throughout an elephant's lifetime. An adult male's tusks grow about 7 inches a year. Tusks are used to dig for salt, water and roots, to debark trees, to clear a path and occasionally in fights. Additionally, they are used for marking trees to establish an elephant's territory.

The elephant's trunk is a fusion of its nose and upper lip. It is the elephant's most important limb. The trunk is sensitive enough to pick up a blade of grass and strong enough to rip the branches off a tree. The trunk is also used for drinking – the elephant can suck up to 14 litres of water at a time and then blow it straight into its mouth!

When bathing, the elephant sucks water to spray on its body. It will then spray dirt and mud on its wet coat, which will dry and act as sunscreen.

Elephants have two gaits – a walk and a faster gait that is similar to running. They cannot jump, trot or gallop, however they can swim and use their trunk as a snorkel.

The elephant has very large ears and they are used to radiate excess heat away from the body.

Elephant has a unique behavior. It is associated with a unique animal intelligence that displays grief, altruism, compassion, self-awareness, play, art and music!

There is a structured social order in the elephant's lifestyle. The females spend their entire lives in tight family groups made up of mothers, grandmothers, aunts, sisters and daughters. The eldest female normally leads the group. Adult males prefer to live a bachelor lifestyle.

They console each other in times of stress by "hugging". According to researchers, elephants hug by putting their trunks in each other's mouths, offering comfort through physical contact.

They Elephants mourn their dead. Wild elephants will stand silently at the bodies of their dead companions, sometimes for days on end. Later, they may return and pay homage to their bones.

They can recognise themselves in a mirror.

That might not sound like a big deal, but humans learn to do this only when we're toddlers, and the only other animals who can do it are dolphins, great apes and magpies.

They live in matriarchal societies. Well, obviously their trunks are like huge, custom-made pointing tools. But most animals haven't mastered this gesture without being taught it, suggesting that elephants are one of the most cognitively advanced species out there.

They can listen with their feet. African elephants can detect rumbling in the ground with sensory cells in their feet. The vibrations travel through their body to their inner ear. They may even use these vibrations to communicate with each other over long distances.

Like us, elephants can get sunburned, so they toss sand over their bodies to protect themselves. They also stop their offspring from getting burnt by standing over them to cast a shadow.

Baby elephants suck their trunks in the same way that human babies suck their thumbs.

Elephants are also environmentally minded, that is because, the circumstances make them in to such reactive animal. And when they get really physically and mentally tortured, then it will certainly take a revenge on that issues.

Elephant needs your help. Given all this evidence about the awesomeness and sensitivity of elephants, it's obvious that taking them away from their families and locking them up is wrong, which is why we need to speak out for them when they are abused and exploited.

Mating & Musth? Do you know? Elephants are the only animals to have a temporal gland. When this gland becomes active the elephant enters a state of behaviour known as musth. In the languages of northern India, musth (originally a Persian word) means a state of drunkenness, hilarity, ecstasy, desire or lust.

Elephants are the only animals to have a temporal gland. When this gland becomes active the elephant enters a state of behaviour known as musth. In the languages of northern India, musth (originally a Persian word) means a state of drunkenness, hilarity, ecstasy, desire or lust.

As lower frequency sounds travel farther than their higher counterparts, their range of communication is extensive. Furthermore, elephants have the ability to judge the distance from another elephant based on the pitch of his/her call. As the sound travels over distances, the higher tones will fade out, leaving a lower pitch.

Zoo elephants reportedly prefer women keepers. They sometimes also masturbate a lot. Describing one female elephant, a zoo keeper told Smithsonian magazine, "Every time you'd turn around, there she'd be, getting off on a log."

Females are only fertile for a few days each year, typically 2-3 days every 14-16 weeks.

They commonly show grief, humor, compassion, cooperation, self-awareness, tool-use, playfulness, and excellent learning abilities.

They are many more interesting facts about this beautiful animal, which you would like to explores. you

There's an easy way to tell the African elephants apart from their Asian cousins – their ears! African elephants have large ears shaped like the continent of Africa! Asian elephants' ears are smaller and shaped like India.

These magnificent mammals spend between 12 to 18 *hours* eating grass, plants and fruit every single day! They use their long trunks to smell their food and lift it up into their mouth – *yum*!

Atention Please!

Helo everyone, This elephant calf wants to talk to you . Listen to him, please!

An elephant calf is requesting another elephant of the herd to protect her. *"I am really scared. Please don't leave me alone. Some people might catch me and take me with them and they will make me do everything using their tough training methods. And with the unbearable pain I have to obey them. Later, they will make me to perform at their circus, Where people come, watch and enjoy. at the cost of our lives. Oh! Please do something. We can not suffer their cruelty any more. Help us. We also love to live peacefully . Will you help me, Please?*

2
Types and Population

Types

There are three types of Elements found in this world.

1. (Loxodonta Africana): An African elephant can grow to 30 ft. (9 meters) from trunk to tail, weigh more than 13,000 lbs. (6 tons/5,442 kilograms) and stand as tall as 12 ft. (4 meters) at the shoulder. The African elephant is classified as Threatened.

2. (Loxodonta cyclones) : Smaller than the African Savanna elephant, the Forest elephant weighs around 5,950 lbs (2.7 tons/2,743 kilograms) and stands up to 8.2 ft. (2.5 meters) at the shoulder. The African Forest elephant is classified as Threatened.

3. (Elephas maximus): An Asian elephant can grow to 18-21 ft. (5.5-6.4 meters) in length, and weigh 4,000-10,000 lbs. (2-5 tons/2000-5000 kilograms) and stand 8-10 ft. at the shoulder (2-3 meters). The Asian elephant is classified as an Endangered Species.

Elephant, (family Elephantidae), largest living land animal, characterized by its long trunk (elongated upper lip and nose), columnar legs, and huge head with temporal glands and wide, flat ears. Elephants are grayish to brown in colour, and their body hair is sparse and coare

African elephants (both species) live in the wild on much of the African continent south of the Sahara. Asian elephants live in the wild in India and Southeast Asia including Sumatra and Borneo. Their former range stretched from the region south of the Himalayas throughout Southeast Asia and into China north to the Yangtze River.

Elephants roam great distances to find enough food and water. Desert elephants, in Africa, migrate almost 300 miles in a year, as far as 35 miles in a day, all in pursuit of water.

They are well-known for living in matriarchal (female-led) social groups, and although elephants are respected and revered by people throughout their ranges in Africa and South Asia, they are also feared because they can be aggressive and dangerous.

Population

According to the World Wide Fund for Nature, in 2014 the total population of African elephants was estimated to be around 700,000. And according to a recent report, the he surviving population of Asian elephants is estimated between 30,000–50,000.

Numbers from different studies vary, but the result is still the same, our elephants are disappearing from the wild.

Total population of the African elephant has markedly dwindled in recent decades, especially in central and eastern Africa. This decline has occurred in the space of a human lifetime and was fuelled by the market for elephant ivory.
Among the African Countries, Botswana has the highest elephant population. According to the latest analysis from counts all over Africa, Botswana has 118,736 wild elephants. On the other hand, Kenya (the safest safari destination) has only 26,427 wild elephants.

India has the most widespread habitat for the elephants, while Sri Lanka has much smaller populations that are greatly restricted to fragmented living areas.

African elephants

African forest elephant

Asian elephant

Elephant Herd at a water source

About Indian Elephant

The Indian elephant is one of the largest land mammals on Earth. The trunk of the Asian elephant has two finger-like structures at its tip that allow the animal to perform both delicate and powerful movements. Elephants have long, coarse hairs sparsely covering their body. Their skin is brown to dark gray.

They have been very important to Asian culture for thousands of years - they have been domesticated and are used for transportation and to move heavy objects. Nothing can compare the majestic build up of an elephant and when you ride on when, it feels like you've gone back to the times of the royal. Indian Elephants always catch the attention of every onlooker, but just like Tigers and Lions this animal has also come under threat of extinction.

Size

Asian elephants stand eight to ten feet tall at the shoulder. Females weigh about 6,000 pounds and males can weigh up to 11,900 pounds! And if they are well looked after their physical features will be more beautiful to look at.

World Elephant Day!
An International Annual Event
on August 12,
dedicated to the preservation and
protection of the world's Elephants
SAVE Elephants

3
Anatomy of an Elephant

Here is the Anatomy of an Elephant the details given below are the facts arrived after a careful study about the physical characteristics of African as well as the Asian elephants.

Age: African elephants can live up to 70 years, and Asian elephants up to 60 years.

All elephants have versatile proboscis or trunk, columnar legs, thick skin (pachydormouse, and sparse patches of hair. Here is the description of physical Structure of Asian Elephant.

Body Weight: An Elephant weighs about 2 500-5500 kg. (4,500-12,000 lbs.)

Body Length: 5.5-6.5 m. (18-21 ft.)

Tail Length / Tail Length: 1.2-1.5 m. (4-5 ft

Shoulder Height: Female: 2.24 m. (8 ft.), Male: 3.2 m. (10 ft.).

Skin: Skin has several textures depending on the location on body –Bumpy skin on most of body, Smooth skin on ears, lips, eyelids, genitalia; Rough texture isn't found in skin of other mammals. The skin of the Asian elephants is generally smoother than the African Elephant's.

Skeleton: As you can see elephant has quite a big skeleton system. The skeleton will weigh about be the weight of the Skeleton \l ton Equals about 15% body weight. Skull weighs equals about 52 kg. (115 lbs.); extensive honeycomb-like spaces reduce skull's weight. Very short neck brings head close to the center of gravity. Cannot turn head side to side

Teeth: Teeth have a high crown with rasp-like surface, which allows them to chew high fiber materials. 26 teeth over lifetime: 2 upper incisors (tusks), 12 deciduous premolars, 12 molars. No canines. Six sets of 4 molars during lifetime.

Average replacement ages are at 1.5 to 2 years, 6 years, 8 to 10 years, 20 to 25 years and at 50 to 6 0 years. The final set is usually lost between 60 and 70 years of age.

Tusks: Function dig for water, salt or rocks, debark trees, serve as weapons, protection or rests for the trunk, move branches. Favors either left or right tusk. One tusk usually shows more wear than the other. Elephant incisors develop into tusks and tusks. Both male and female African elephants usually have tusks. Tusks barely extend past the mouth; replaced by permanent tusks.

Trunk: Technical term is "proboscis," meaning "before the mouth" (Greek) It is a tool for tool for lifting, smelling, spraying dust, grass, and water on body. Used to transfer water to mouth, not used like a drinking straw. It is also used for sound

Ears: Asian elephants have Smaller than the African elephants. Thermo regulation - positive correlation between the number of times an elephant flaps its ears and air temperature. Can hear approximately 8Hz. – 12 kHz

Glands: Two mammary glands produce milk that is 83.82% water, 11.82% albuminoids and sugar, 3.89% fat and 0.47% ash or mineral matter. Cheek (temporal) glands located midway between eyes and ears. Drain during times of excitement such as fighting, mating or in musth (once or twice a year. Present in both males and females; much more active in males. Tear ducts are vestigial. Herderian glands lubricate the eyes.

Eyesight: Eye is small in relation to body size. Ability to see color - probably similar to humans who are color blind. Total visual field is a sweep of 313° out of 360° with a 47°

blind spot. Good in dull light, considerably reduced in bright light.'

Sexual Dimorphism: Males have large trunk bases, bulges below and in front of eyes, and swelling above the eyes. Females have narrower trunk bases and lack prominent bulge above eyes. Male back is more convex and curves more gradually into hindquarters; female's is straighter and "boxier" with vertical hindquarters. Males considerably larger than females of same ages.

Nothing can compare the majestic buildup of an elephant and when you ride on when, it feels like you've gone back to the times of the royal. Indian Elephants always catch the attention of every onlooker, but just like Tigers and Lions this animal has also come under threat of extinction.

Senior member of a herd along with other elephants mourn at the death of a member of their Herd

An elephant calf looking for her mother?

Elephants mating

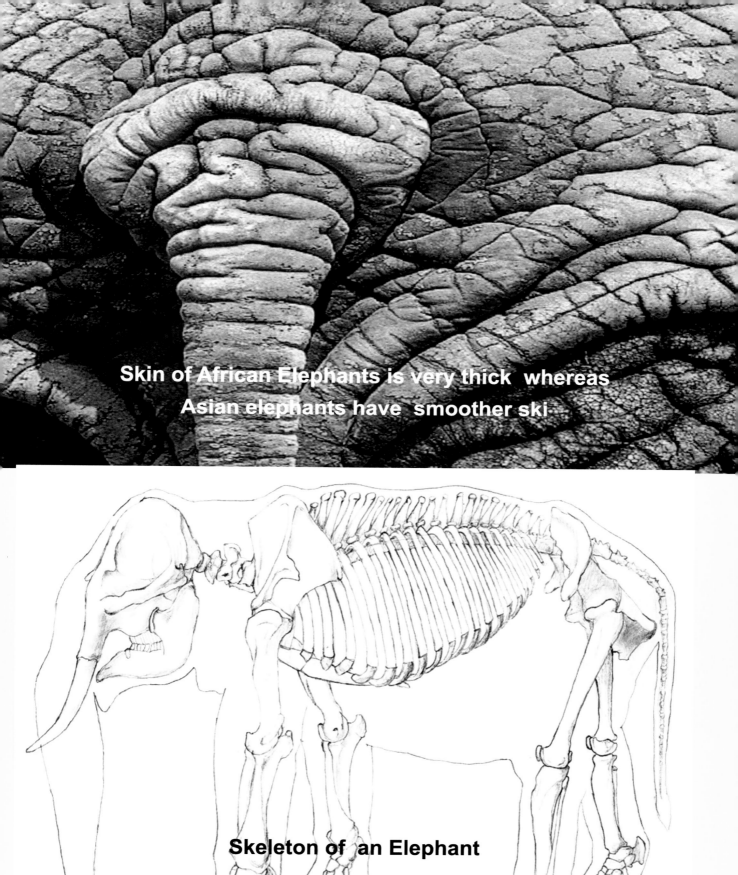

Skin of African Elephants is very thick whereas
Asian elephants have smoother ski

Skeleton of an Elephant

Life and Behavior

Life and Behavior

4
Life and Behavior

Life

Elephants are mammals of the family Elephantidae and the largest existing land animals. Three species are currently recognise: the African bush elephant, the African forest elephant, and the Asian elephant. Elephantidae is the only surviving family of the order Proboscidea; extinct members include the mastodons.

The family Elephantidae also contains several now-extinct groups, including the mastodons and straight-tusked elephants. African elephants have larger ears and concave backs, whereas Asian elephants have smaller ears, and convex or level backs. Distinctive features of all elephants include a long trunk, tusks, large ear flaps, massive legs, and tough but sensitive skin.

The trunk, also called a mastodons, is used for breathing, bringing food and water to the mouth, and grasping objects. Tusks, which are derived from the incisor teeth, serve both as weapons and as tools for moving objects and digging.

The large ear flaps assist in maintaining a constant body temperature as well as in communication. The pillar -like legs carry their great weight. Elephants are scattered throughout and are found in different habitats, sub-Saharan Africa, South Asia, and Southeast Asia including savannahs, forests, deserts, and marshes.

They are herbivorous, and they stay near water when it is accessible. They are considered to be keystone species, due to their impact on their environments. Other animals tend to keep their distance from elephants; the exception is their predators such as lions, tigers, hyenas, and wild dogs, which usually target only young elephants (calves).

Elephants have a fission–fusion society, in which multiple family groups come together to socialise. Females (cows) tend to live in family groups, which can consist of one female with her calves or several related females with offspring. The groups, which do not include bulls, are led by the (usually) oldest cow, known as the matriarch.

Males (bulls) leave their family groups when they reach puberty, and may live alone or with other males. Adult bulls mostly interact with family groups when looking for a mate. They enter a state of increased testosterone and aggression known as musth, which helps them gain dominance over other males as well as reproductive success. Calves are the Centre of attention in their family groups and rely on their mothers for as long as three years.

Elephants can live up to 70 years in the wild. They communicate by touch, sight, smell, and sound; elephants use infrasound, and seismic communication over long distances. Elephant intelligence has been compared with that of primates andcetaceans . They appear to have self-awareness, as well as appearing to show empathy for dying and dead family members.

African elephants are listed as savannahs, and Asian elephants as savannah, by the savannahs, (IUCN). One of the biggest threats to elephant populations is the ivory trade, as the animals are ivory trade for their ivory tusks. Other threats to wild elephants include habitat destruction and conflicts with local people. Elephants are used as working animals in Asia. In the past, they were used in war; today, they are often controversially put on display in zoos, or exploited for entertainment in circuses. Elephants are highly recognizable and have been featured in art, folklore, religion, literature, and popular culture.

Groups of elephants, or herds, follow a matriarchal structure with the eldest female in charge. Herds are composed of primarily female family members and young calves, according to the San Diego Zoo, and include 6 to 20 members depending on the food supply. When the family gets too large, herds often split into smaller groups that stay within the same area.

The matriarch relies on her experience and memory to recall where the best spots for food, water are, and where to find protection from the elements. The matriarch is also responsible for teaching the younger members of her family how to socialize with other elephants.

Savannahs, and can communicate with one another and identify other elephants from distances of up to 2 miles using rumbling, low-pitched sounds that fall below the audible range of humans, according to the National Zoo. Savannahs, Elephants also pay close attention to the well-being of all the members of their herd, and will do what they can to take care of and protect weak or injured members.

They're considered an extremely intelligent species have been observed showing advanced problem-solving skills and demonstrating empathy, mourning and self-awareness, according to an article published in US.

Behavior of Indian Elephants

Elephants live in a matriarchal family group of related females called a herd. They are led by the oldest and often largest female in the herd. Herds consist of eight to 100 individuals. Males may be associated with a herd, solitary or may live temporarily with other males. Elephants produce a variety of sounds including low frequency calls, high pitched calls and loud trumpeting.

Indian Elephants - Food

Asian elephants eat grass, bark, roots and leaves. They also like crops such as banana grown by farmers, making them a pest in agricultural areas. Adult elephants eat about 330 pounds of food a day. They must drink water every day and are never far from a water source.

Maturity

Male and female elephants become sexually mature between 8 and 13 years of age. Male elephants will leave their herd around this time, as long as they're able to find their own food and protect themselves, according to the Smithsonian National Zoo. Adult males either live on their own or in small bachelor herds.

Musth and Mating!

Elephants are the only animals to have a temporal gland. When this gland becomes active the elephant enters a state of behaviour known as musth. In the languages of northern India, musth (originally a Persian word) means a state of drunkenness, hilarity, ecstasy, desire or lust.

Musth is a condition unique to elephants, which has still not been scientifically explained. It affects sexually mature male elephants usually between the ages of 20 and 50. It occurs annually and lasts for a period of between 2-3 weeks in the wild, usually during the hot season. During this time, the elephant becomes highly agitated, aggressive and can be dangerous. Even normally placid animals have been known to kill people and other elephants when in the full throes of musth. It generally lasts 4 to 6 weeks in captivity but has been said to have lasted as long as 2 months.

The reasons for its occurrence are not fully understood. The animal is sexually agitated, but musth is not thought to be entirely sexual in nature. Elephants mate outside the musth period and it is not the same as the rutting season common in some other mammals. When in musth, a strong-smelling oily secretion flows from a gland above the eye and elephants will also constantly dribble urine.

The temporal gland discharge can be quite free flowing and run down the elephants face dripping down their chin. While in musth everything changes with the elephant; the way they walk, their interactions with other elephants, the degree of aggression, and as mentioned, the odor they exude. In rare circumstances, if two male elephants in musth cross paths the ensuing fight can turn into a fight to the death.

It is difficult to describe just how extreme musth can affect an elephants' normal disposition. Captive elephants experiencing musth are usually kept securely chained or isolated and managed from a distance until the torment subsides, after which they will return to their usual character.

Historically, captive male elephants in musth have been chained by all four legs, with chains from their tusks down to their feet, and from tusk to tusk in front of their trunks to prevent them from lunging with their heads and swinging their trunks at trainers. From the age of 45-50 musth gradually diminishes, eventually disappearing altogether. On very exceptional occasions, a form of musth has been recorded in females but little is known about its purpose.

Both sexes may become sexually mature at as early as 9 years, but males usually do not reach sexual activity until 14-15 years, and even if, they are not capable of the social dominance that usually is necessary for successful reproductive activity. There is usually competition among the males for females that are in estrus.

If there is a male in musth present around females in estrus, non-musth males will generally back away from the competition; the level of testosterone in a musth male creates an unmatched degree of anger, aggression and strength. Often more than one male will gather around the area of a female that is ready to breed, and the most dominant male is the one who is allowed to carry out breeding. This can be decided peacefully, especially if the size and strength difference is obvious, or sometimes the elephants will fight over that rite.

Females may not have their first calf until their middle teen years, while males may not father a calf until they are in their 30s, when they are large and strong enough to compete with other males, according to the National Zoo.

Usually, only a single calf is born following a 22-month pregnancy. A newborn calf weighs between 150 and 350 lbs. (68 and 158 kg) stands about 3 feet tall. Calves also tend to be hairy with long tails and very short trunks.

Elephant calves grow quickly, gaining 2 to 3 lbs. every day in their first year, according to the San Diego Zoo. By the time they are 2 or 3 years old, calves are ready to be weaned.

In the wild, elephants can live to be about 70 years old. In a survey of 4,500 captive elephants worldwide, among African elephants, zoo-born females live an average of 16.9 years in zoos, while those in the wild make it to 56. Asian elephants, the more endangered of the two species, live 18.9 years in captivity and 41.7 in the wild. (Time 2008).

Captive elephants suffer from chronic health problems such as tuberculosis, arthritis, and foot abscesses, which nearly always lead to premature death.

5
Elephant in Captivity and Training

The tradition of training elephants goes back some 4 000 years, developed in the Hindu valley, as far as the oldest paintings and statues document. All over southeast Asia the traditions of catching and training wild elephants spread. In most cases the elephants were possessed by rich kings, for war or prestige, and the trainers formed into particular castes, trained and disciplined by superior trainers in the king's elephants' stables, forming the elephant cavalries.

Originally, an art of hunting tribes, that used to capture elephants now and then, it became a profession, where knowledge was handed down from old generations to younger. In large stables the riders were soldiers, and organized like a cavalry. Elephants were caught with lassos from tame elephants (mela) trapped in pits, or scared into large pallisades (Keddha).

After the capture of elephants, only the most promising animals are selected for training. They would be roped, and pulled out from the Keddha, with help of specially trained elephants called Kungkhies. After a period in a Kraal, a cage with wooden bars, were the elephants could be approached in safety, and where the first contact was made with food, water and rewards, as well as punishment for aggressiveness, the elephants would undergo training with Kungkhies and experienced mahouts.

Training included being overpowered and pulled down in lying position with help of ropes, but there was less hitting than what people in general expect. The more an elephant gets hit during this period, the more dangerous is the work for the trainer, and the longer time it will take to reach a stage, where the trainer can approach the elephant, and stand beside it, without being attacked.

The sooner the captured elephant starts to cooperate, the sooner the work gets safer for the mahouts, and the training progress develops. After some three or four months, the captured elephants would be taken to work with other tamed elephants. And this tradition slowly spread towards the west.

The Europeans was trained by Asian mahouts, often from Sri Lanka, and a mixture between the Asian mahouts, and the German horse trainers mentality formed the western elephant trainer, while in America, a major part of elephant trainers had a stronger circus affiliation

In 1900, there was a fast development of imports of elephant for circuses and shows in Zoos. This was a rough time for elephants, and even if the training methods only seldom were as brutal as animal welfare people describe them, the elephants suffered from bad food, cold weather, lacking of "normal" mental stimuli and possibilities to perform natural behaviours, but already now they started to breed.

The keeper learned actually from the elephants, in a trail-and-error way what was working and what was not. This was a method that had been used now and then in Asia before, and it was an application from the stage when the elephants were trained in the Kraal.
The majority of elephants, though, adapted very well to the captive situation in Zoos, and the training was not their problem, the health problems were more on arthritis, food related, or fights between the elephants, accidents and falling down in moats. Especially foot problems caused a lot of suffering, especially in Off-hand situations. Training is mainly based on a mixture of old Asian methods, and circus training.

Captive Elephants suffer from chronic health problems such as tuberculosis, arthritis, and foot abscesses, which nearly always lead to premature death.

Elephants are highly social animals, and the stress of captivity often results in shortened life spans.In the wild, elephants move constantly, migrating as much as 30 miles per day, and are active for 18 hours a day. Zoo's lack of space creates health problems in elephants, such as muscular-skeletal ailments, arthritis, foot and joint diseases, tuberculosis, reproductive problems, high infant mortality rates, obesity, and psychological distress.

6

Elephant as Working Animal

Elephants are employed to do many tasks. In earlier days they were used in road building to pull wagons and push boulders.

In the captivity, elephants are trained sufficient enough to make them to perform and they are then employed by the owner for executing his own tasks or give his elephants on daily rent to anyone who wants to avail the services of an elephant.

Thus, elephants are used for Timber logging, where the elephants use their tusks and trunks to move big logs where ever they wanted them to.

Later, elephants are also used for 'elephant tourism' like, Trekking, Elephants and Safaris, in Zoos, in Circus and in Temples and Festivals.

Elephants in Temples and Festivals

It is centuries old practice to use elephants in various temple ceremonies and festivals. And the number of elephants participating and the actual conduct of the festivals will all be decided by the temple administrative board Devaswam all depended on the size and financial situation of the temples.

Participating in Temple Festivals is much more tiring and fatigue to the elephants. Elephants are used mainly in religious parades carrying effigies of Hindu Gods and they are sometimes dressed in gold for religious festivals and marriage processions.

In order to hire an elephant for a temple festival, you have to pay the daily rent for the elephant plus you also have to pay additional charges for transporting the elephant from the elephant owner 's location to the temple location and back. Elephants are transported in big trucks. This adds additional strain to the elephants and also the risk of accidents en-route. Now you can imagine, elephants standing all the way, like standing in a cage, chained, with lot of stress and strain while the driver managing the truck during driving.

Temple Culture.

What actually happens at the temple festivals? Elephants are dressed up, during the display of colourful parasols, which generally last for of one hour minimum. But in the case of Thrissur Pooram festival, the elephants from both the temples, Paremakkave and Thruwmambadi Devaswam Boards, temples sides of are lined up for display from about 4.30 p. m onwards till about 6.30 - 7p.m pm or so during which a big event called *Kudamattom* will take place. Meaning both the temple side will change beautiful, colourful umbrellas, sometime there will be about 10 to 15 type, each side changes. And the number and type and shape of the umbrellas increase every year. This, prolongs the display period.

Indeed, this event is really a feast to the onlookers and it is gaining popularity, and attracts many tourists, not only from other parts of India but also from abroad. No doubt, it is one of the great festivals where the Indian temple culture is showcased to the world. Form the pictures given here, you can see how beautifully the elephants are dressed with shining face lift along with other items held on them by other men.

But for the elephants, it really a punishment. Because they have to stand in the same spot with very limited movements for about 3 to 4 hours at a time and two to three similar Poorams of lesser duration. So, you can very well imagine the condition of the elephants coming from far off places in trucks, the participate in the Pooram, and may be some of them have next assignment waiting them for the next day.

We can understand that some of the temple culture are centuries old. For example, Thrissur Pooram was started by *Shakthan Thamburan*, during AD1800, who was the Ruler of this area.

But what about other temples, which came into existence much later. And we find no connection with the elephants and the temple culture, its all man-made rituals to add more   colour to the celebrations. We must realise the physical and mental torture the elephant torture he goes through. But being an animal generally it doesn't' react. But the situation crosses the limit, where the elephant cannot bear any more cruelty, it turns violent. And sometime it runs amok.

World Elephant Day
is an international annual event
on August 12,
dedicated to the preservation
and protection of the world's elephants.
Please do whatever you can and
SAVE Elephants

Elephant as Working Animal

Elephants performing at a Circus

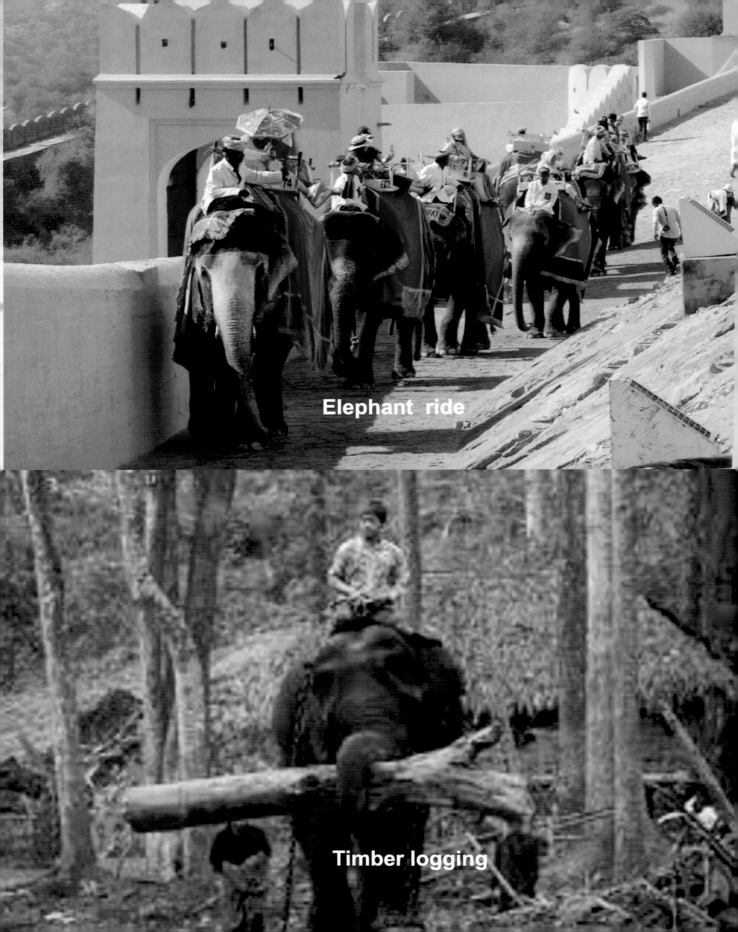

Elephant ride

Timber logging

Elephant ride

Timber logging

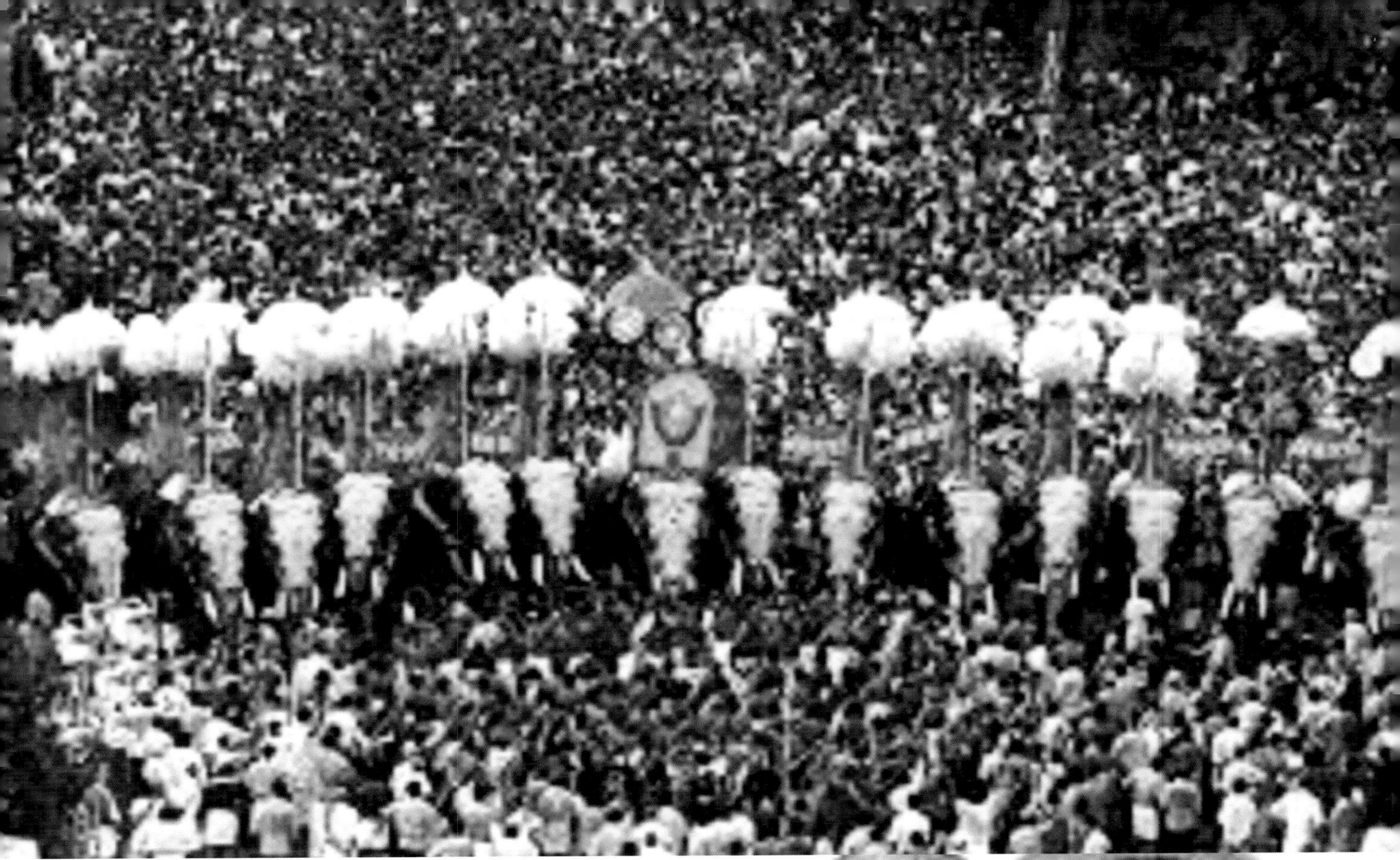

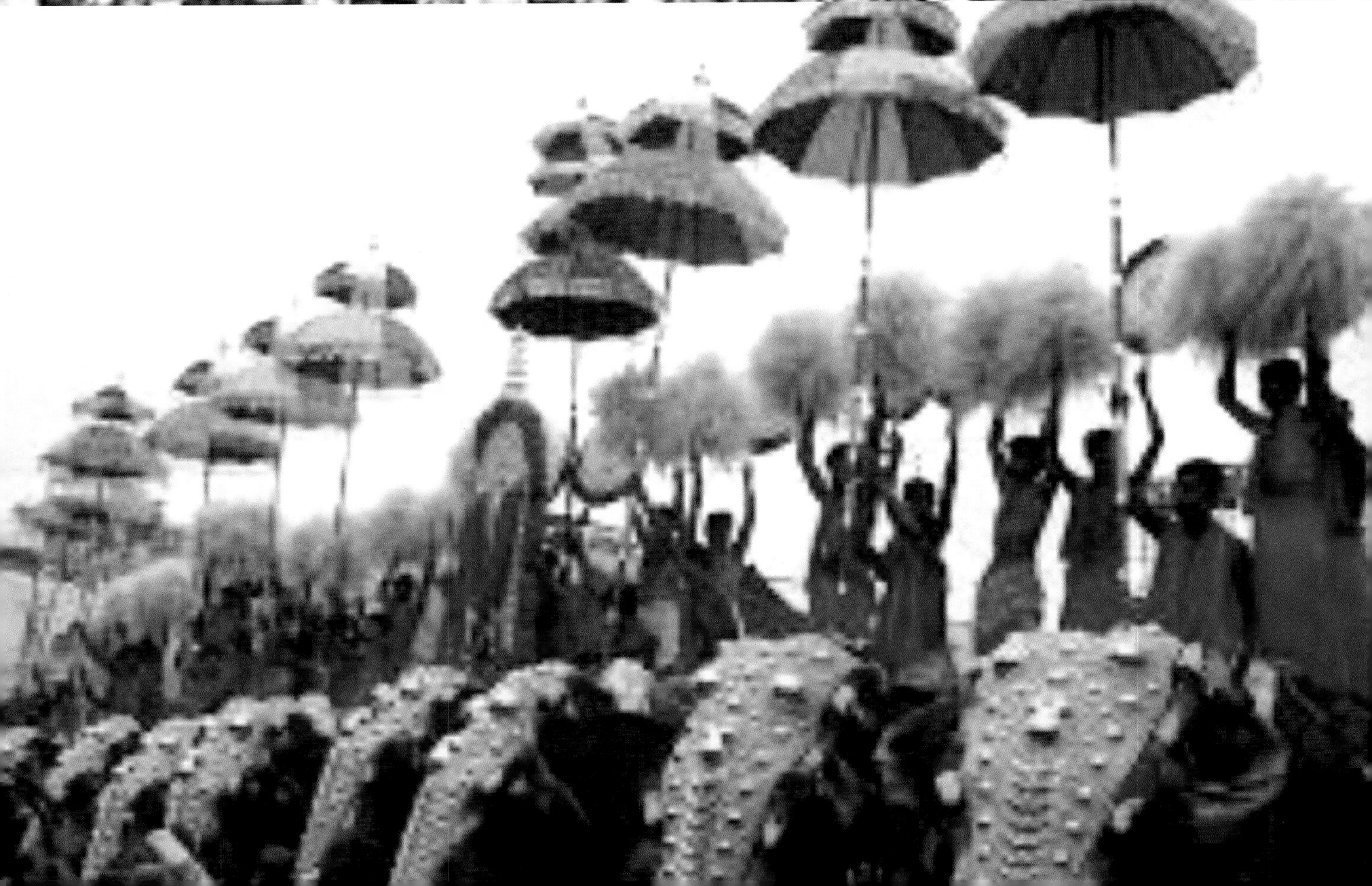

7

Elephant Your Pet!

Two Brothers in Kerala have Elephants as their pets?

Passion for Pets

You know, sometime back, may be a couple of years back, a young man from our neighborhood asked me, "Uncle, do you have any pets?

My wife and me were working in our house garden. On hearing this, my wife smiled at me. Even I couldn't resist a smile on my face.

When someone ask me about my pet dogs, I become very emotional and excited, which he had noticed.

The guy was listening to me with great interest .

So, with a big smile I replied him. "well, I like pets, my family like pets. And you know, we have been having pet dogs since 1970 till 2018 and we have had 12 pet dogs of different breeds."

And then I showed him a picture where I had made a mosaic with the pictures of all our pet dogs. Then I showed a picture of our last two pet dogs we had, a pair of Labradors, Bruno and Lyka.
"They have also left us, Lyka in December 2015 and Bruno in April 2017", I added.

I continued, "Do you know, we have had12 Pet dogs in a period of 48 years, and during this period we have travelled with our pet dogs over a total distance of 43,500 kilometers by our car in first class cabin with us. But I had never put them in the dogs cage kept in the Train Guard's cabin. Because I loved them, we loved them so much. In fact, they were not just Pet Dogs for us; they were part of our family.

"But Uncle, I heard that you were in the Army. So how could you keep pet dogs with you?"

Listening to his second question, my first reaction was "What is that this guy is trying to find out?" But then, I didn't want to hurt him. On the other hand, in my mind, I appreciated his confidence to ask me such a question and his interest to learn more about it.

So, I simply asked him, "what is you want to know?" I found him little hesitant to talk further. "Don't you worry. You can tell me." I told him.

Then he said, "Uncle, our family has moved in here two weeks back. I like pets and I want to get some pet. In fact, I asked the uncle living next to our house. He is the one who told me about you. He said many things about you uncle, about your pet dogs, birds, about some of the books you have written and published. So I wanted to ask you something about the pet I want to keep."

At this, my wife told him. "That's ok. You can talk to Uncle and ask whatever you want and he will he help you out." And she looked at me.

"Ok. Come in. let us sit down and talk." And I pulled the garden chairs.

"Come sit. Btw, what's your name?"

As I started talking about our pets, I realised, he also wanted to keep a pet dog. He wanted to know everything. How to take care of a puppy and make him avery good pet dog.

I knew. if I have to explain everything in detail to him it would have taken lot of time. So, decided to tell him everything in brief.

"You know, all our pet dogs had come in to our family when they were about 20 to 30 days old puppies. I cared them. Of course, my wife and our two children, always helped me. I trained them, each one of them into a beautiful, well trained dogs. They were always with us. They had full freedom to move around in our house. And each one had their own place where they would rest. I wanted our pet dogs to be friendly with our family members. At the same time they should create fear and scare in anyone other than our family members. I tried to explain other things very briefly, like about their food, and how to feed them etc.

He was so keen. He kept asking for more details and clearing his doubts. After a while. my wife came with some coffee, looked at me and asked me, " Are you going to tell him everything, including "The Unforgettable Moments we spent together with our children, during the 48 years of our association?

Only then I realised that it was already very late. So, I told him, "Try and recollect everything I explained to you today. And we shall continue our discussion later. Ok?"

After he left, it was a beautiful recollection of our past. Every moment of our life was a memorable moment.

Believe it or not, even now at 74 years of my age, my life is full of activities. Though I have many ailments, my activities keep them away from me and let me move forward. Even at this age my creative ideas and innovative thinking make my life, our life more beautiful.

It is my attitude that made me what I m today. As a published author, I have many books to my credit under different categories They are all available online anytime, anywhere in this world. In addition to this, I also have many hobbies and social network

Now, I would like to ask each one of you,

Do you like Pets? And do you have any pets at your home?

Btw, what is your ultimate idea of a pet? Cats, dogs, birds, ornamental fish, rabbits... your list might end there. But can you imagine an elephant standing in your courtyard flapping its ears?

Here, certainly I would like to share something very interesting and informative I read in the Internet, very recently.

If you still can't charge your imagination to draw a picture like that, then come to Mangalamkunnu a small province in the village of Sreekrishnapuram in the district of Palakkad. Here, you will find fourteen tuskers in and around a house relaxing and relishing the food and love offered by their owners - Parameswaran and Haridas.

xxxxxxx

Quote form the website

*"For brothers Parameswaran and Haridas of Mangalamkunnu, popularly known as Mangalamkunnu brothers, **elephants are family pets**. At present they are the largest individual owners of elephants in Kerala, next only to Guruvayoor Devaswom. The Mangalamkunnu brothers stepped in to the world of elephants in 1978 when they bought an elephant from Uttar Pradesh, which they named as Ayyappankutty.*

Since then, they have been purchasing an elephant once in every two years and their family Mangalamkunnu Tharavadu gradually came to be known as Aana Tharavadu (Elephant Home)."

Earlier, the elephants were bought from the northeastern states of India like Bihar and Assam. But presently buying elephants have become a costly affair especially after some restrictions were imposed in the trade of elephants.

The Mangalamkunnu family doesn't want to see elephants as a source of income. It is their love for this giant peace-loving animal that prompts them to stay in the field. Because of their love for the elephants they are against deputing their jumbos for heavy works like pulling of logs.

The prices stood at Rs 10 lakh a decade ago. The turning point was in 2007-08, when a deal was struck for Rs 27 lakh, says Dr Giridas.

More than profit, it is the sheer passion for these animals that has driven Haridas and Parameshwar to own so many elephants. *But since owning an elephant now costs more than what it takes to buy a super-luxury car, the owners are leaving no stone unturned in providing the right care for the big animals.*

xxxxxxxx quote ends.

Here, I have my own views. If I were in such a situation, whatever be the type of animals, big or small, I will never allow my pet animals to be away from me, whatever renumeration I might get, or people offer me in return.

Now I am wondering, having many years of experience in training my pet dogs, 12 of them from their puppy stage till they are fully grown and managed them, till they died reaching their old age, I am quite confident that I can certainly train an elephant calf. I am not joking, if someone can spare/ make it available one elephant baby calf, I will be too happy, to train the calf please, Anyone willing?

You can train your pet animals without beating/ punishing them. Here is yet another point I want to share you that while training our pet dogs, I have never used any cane to beat/ scare my pet dogs or I have ever beaten them. But we always understood each other's language. They had always identified the tone of all my voice command, and they could also read my eyes. I had trained them with all possible voice command which we all like our pet dogs to obey.

Animals are intelligent too. Another point we are generally under the impression that animals are not intelligent. But I must say that we are wrong. There are many wonderful intelligent birds and animals, living in this world. And dogs are one among them, our dogs used to watch our TV, especially when we play their video. Form what we observed, they can identify them on the screen and we have seen them enjoying the TV program.

These Picture are of our Pet Dog's family.

I trained all my Pet Dogs
without a cane

Dimple Jr.

Dimple

Hero

Juno

Juno

Patty

Lyka

Dolly

Lyka J

Patty Jr.

Our Pets were very intelligent too .They could identify themselves on the TV screeen

Lyka enjoying her video on our TV

Bruno enoing a drive with me

Lyka can even regonise me

8

Elephant Rental - A Roaring Business

The craze for participating elephants for the temple functions and number of elephants taking part, are all becoming a prestige issue. More the number, and taller the elephants, people are very happy. But getting into such a competitive spirit, increases the demand for elephants.

Earlier, People owned elephants for their own use like, if a timber merchant, elephants were used for logging or rent them out to others. And renting elephants for the temple ceremonies and other festivals was one among them.

Keeping **elephants** and **renting** them out for Temple ceremonies and for other 'festivals has grown into booming business in the recent years. An average tusker of fine features can fetch a **rent** of between Rs30,000 and Rs 80,000 a day and if your elephant is quite tall with very good features, it can fetch you even one crore or may be even more. Sounds quite unbelievable!   Well, it is true.

Many Festivals - A few Elephants.

Parades of bedecked elephants bearing idols and colourful parasols are a common sight during the temple festival season in Kerala. According to some unofficial estimates, more than 500 such festivals are held during this season.

Animal rights groups say the festival season puts a huge amount of pressure on the captive elephants in the state, who do not receive adequate rest for several months at a time.

One of the reasons for this is because the number of elephants in the state have declined in the past 10 years while the number of temple festivals has gone up.

The increase in the number of festivals puts pressure on the animals as these 400 elephants have to grace more than 500 festivals, says the founder of the Heritage Animal Task Force, a Thrissur-based non-governmental organisation working to prevent cruelty towards animals.

The number of elephants used in each festival ranges from five to 120. In 2018, as many as 117 elephants were part of the Thrissur Pooram parade.

Owners get Rs 3 lakh a day for every elephant they rent out, It said. The huge amount of money at stake means owners even rent out elephants when they are in musth – a periodic condition in male elephants, when a surge in reproductive hormones makes them aggressive, which sometimes leads to the loss of lives. This condition can last a few weeks or months.

What a profitable business! No wonder why more people are falling into this category of business. You can never think of a such a profitable business in this world today. So, are you also thinking of buying some elephants and become an owner of some elephants and start an Elephant Rental business?

Sonepur Animal Market - major source for Elephant Buy / Sell

But this the existing ban on capture of wild elephants and year, the ban on trading elephants at the Sonepur aniimal markt, terdingBut this the existing ban on capture of wild elephants and year, the ban on trading elephants at the Sonepur aniimal markt, terding

9

Ban on Use of Animals - World Reacts

United Kingdom, Romania, Netherlands, Iran and a number of U.S cities have already passed laws banning the use of wild animals in circuses setting a precedent for others to follow.

In welcome move, no circus in India can now make wild animals perform tricks

The ministry deregistered several circuses under the Prevention of Cruelty to Animals Act, 1960, to ban the training, exhibition and use of elephants for performances.

The days of elephants standing on two legs or balancing themselves on beach balls to entertain India's circus enthusiasts are over. The ministry of environment, forests and climate change (MoEFCC) has passed orders cancelling the recognition of all circuses across the country that make wild animals perform tricks.

In India *no circus is any longer recognised* by the governing body as they were found to violate the laws with regard to basic standards of food, adequate shelter and veterinary care for animals that were used in tricks and performances. The recognition of Zoo Rules, 2009 laid down prerequisite conditions for zoo animals to be met by circuses. These included sufficient space for each animal, proper waste management, medical care and no exhibition of ailing animals.

In spite of a 2013 ban on the use of elephants, the animal was still found to be used in some circuses and the operators to save their face came up with a fake story stating that the elephants were used only for educational purposes. These elephants when rescued could not even move due to injuries they received during training and while being extensively chained.

In spite of a 2013 ban on the use of elephants, the animal was still found to be used in some circuses and the operators to save their face came up with a fake story stating that the elephants were used only for educational purposes. These elephants when rescued could not even move due to injuries they received during training and while being extensively chained.

In India at Sonepur, in Bihar, there is is an animal market for trading almost all types of animals. Sonepur is the place where an annual market for trading all types of animals, including Animal Market held during every November where trading fo all kinds of animals takes place including Elephants.

So far this has been the major source for bringing elephants from other states into Kerala. But now as i said, the existing ban on capturing wild elephants , training them and with the ban on trading of elephants at the Sonepur Animal market will make the situation further still worse and the demand for the captive elephants will further increase.

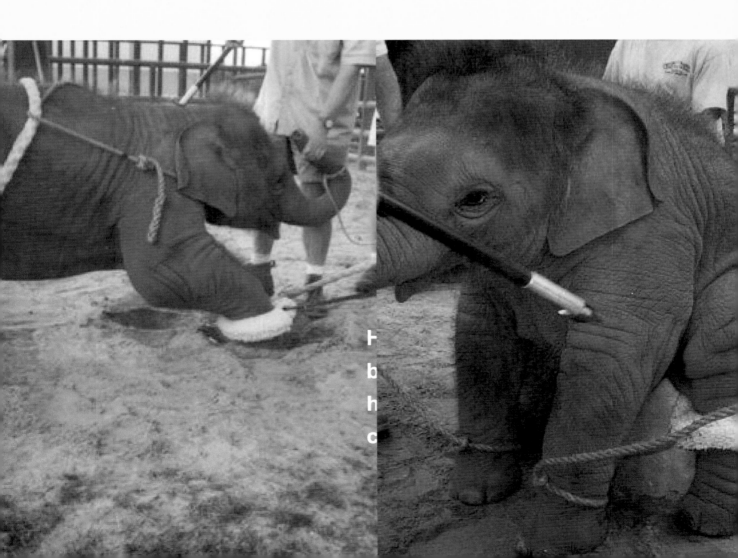

gettyimages

10

Elephant Poaching

Poaching is the illegal taking of wildlife, in violation of local, state, federal, or international law. Activities that are considered poaching include killing an animal out of season, without a license, with a prohibited weapon, or in a prohibited manner. Killing a protected species, exceeding one's bag limit, or killing an animal while trespassing is also considered poaching.

The illegal killing of elephants in sub-Saharan Africa began to rise in 2005. Many scientists suspected the rise was due to growing demand for ivory in China, where carved ivory has long been treasured and a growing middle class was flush with cash. It developed into a huge poaching problem. By 2014, the continental population of savanna elephants had dropped by almost a third to an estimated 352,000. To figure out which elephants were killed by poachers—and which died of natural causes—rangers working with the Convention on International Trade in Endangered Species of Wild Fauna and Flora examined carcasses found at 53 sites in parks across the continent. Their annual reports cover about half the African elephant population.

An updated assessment by a United Nations Environment Programme-administered treaty has confirmed that poaching continues to threaten the long-term survival of the African elephants. So what should we do?

11

Animal Abuse

Animal Rights, Protection and Welfare

Captive elephants are generally under the control of the Wild Life Department of the local government and under the private ownership of individuals. And each country will/ should have Rules and Regulations passed in regard to Captive Elephants of their countries. about the ownership, their care and maintenance, minimum area for living, food, water, health, etc. And if it is a working elephant how long you can make them work, rest during the working hours, and in case, you have to transport an elephant, how to transport them, all such details will be covered under the regulations.

All that you / the elephant owners need to do is just follow the instructions, correctly. As long as you comply with those regulations there shall no problem either to you or to the elephants. But if you are not, following those regulations fully, then, action can be initiated against you for, animal protection, cruelty of animals.

What is happening around the world?

Unauthorised capturing of wild elephant continues. In addition, other activities like, poaching elephants for their Ivory, cruelty/ ill treatment, then their restless life style especially while capturing, training and using them in temples and festivals are really on the increase., in a way beyond control.

In some countries, for example like in India, use of elephants for their temple festival are on the increase. As of today, during the festive season, there will be around 400 temple festivals in the small state of Kerala alone. And since the number of elephants is declining every year, the available elephants have to manage these temple festivals, sometime travelling from one temple festival to another, not getting enough rest in between.

Long journeys in shackles

The festival season is also particularly stressful for elephants because they have to be transported from one venue to another. For this, they are often loaded onto trucks and shackled, and have to remain that way on long road journeys without much sleep or food.

Animal rights activists say inadequate food and rest affects the digestive system and lungs of elephants and eventually kills them. More than 30 elephants have died in the last 18 months," said an activist on condition of anonymity.

Careless handling of animals and negligence by truck drivers have also hurt many elephants. On April 14, 2019, an elephant suffered deep gashes on his forehead after the driver of the truck the animal was being transported in went to fill fuel. drove the vehicle into the petrol pump without taking into account the height of the roof [of the petrol pump]," the mahout said. What a pitty

The latest craze!

Temple festivals are now celebrated with a competitive spirit among the local community. There by, every year, they try to do well over others, by increasing the number of elephants taking part in the festival.

Even some *churches in Kerala have also started participating elephants for their church festival, something never heard off in the past.* Not one, two or three but, it is in 10, 20 and 30s.

It has no connection between elephants, bible or their belief. Elephants are also used for film shooting, and the event managers use them for marriages and for inauguration of shops etc. thus making the life of elephants more difficult. All these are nothing but Abuse of Elephant.

But it is the daily rental value, the elephant owner gets for the elephants he owns making people crazy, thus, making the elephants as a money -making tools. Food, free movements, treatment in case of any illness. Injury, all become secondary.

Another important point is as long as the elephants are healthy to perform the duties assigned to them, the owner will be very happy, Bu, when the elephants become old or become very sick, what happens to such elephants? Maintenance of the elephants including the treatment, being very expensive, you won't be surprised if such elephants are put to sleep and encash their remaining wealth on their body they are carrying like valuable Tusks (Ivory) and other items like hair, etc.

Elephant ride:

Several studies show the extent and scale of this suffering of captive elephants in varying situations in India. *There are 116 elephants at Amer Fort in Jaipur in Rajasthan who suffer chronic stress, heat and physical abuse.* Abuse is rife among the elephants in Jaipur, who endure repeated beatings, inadequate diet and long hours of work. The elephants have to walk down the hard surface of a road, for which their feet are not suited. Rajasthan is not a natural elephant range state.

Elephant Protection

Every country is concerned / worried about the animals in their country. And each country generally has its own regarding the animal protection and welfare of their animals, whether, wild domestic. A far as s India is concerned, a major cause of concern is: According to the Wildlife Protection Society of India, in last five years alone, India has lost nearly 100 elephants in train-related accidents.

12

Elephant Tourism – Future Trends

Elephant tourism is a highly debated topic for the millions of travelers seeking wildlife experiences yearly. While traditionally viewed as a romanticized way of connecting with Asian wildlife, modern day research has proven that the activity may not be ethically sound after all.

Besides elephant riding and trekking being extremely harmful to an elephant's already damaged spine (from cage-induced stunted growth and abuse), trekking baskets also cause sores that are often left barely treated.

It has been found that in many of these 'Sanctuaries" elephants have been taken from their natural habitats, held captive, and emotionally and physically abused in order to "crush the spirit" (a hill tribe practice to break in" elephants to submission). On the other hand, there are a small number of parks that rescue these elephants from circuses, illegal trade, and harmful environments by purchasing the victim elephants themselves.

In India and Nepal, elephants are widely used on safaris that look for tigers and rhinos and to take tourists to tourist spots. Female elephants are preferred to male ones. Of the 97 elephants used to carry tourist up a hill to a popular fort in Jaipur India only nine are males. The reason is sex. One tourism official told AP, "the bulls often fight among themselves while they are carrying tourists on their backs. Because of biological demand, the bull elephant in rut often and becomes bad-tempered. In one case an aggressive male pushed a female into a ditch while it was carrying two foreign tourists. The tourists were unhurt but the female elephant died from her injuries.

Elephants and Trekking:

Elephant Trekking is very popular in Thailand, especially in the Chiang Rai area. Trekkers usually ride on wooden platforms that are tied to the backs of the elephants, who are amazingly sure footed on the steep, narrow and sometimes slippery trails. The mahouts sit on the elephants' neck and guide the animals by nudging a sensitive area behind their ears with a stick while the trekkers sway back and forth in a firm, steady motion.

When riding on an elephant you can feel the raised spine and rumbling movement of the shoulder blades. Sometimes, people-carrying elephants in Thailand stop on the trail to snack on leaves and plants and tourist try to urge them to get a swat from the trunk and spray of water.

Elephants and Safaris

Elephants have a penchant for retrieving fallen or lost objects such as lens caps, ballpoint pens, binoculars etc. You know, most elephants are very intelligent, alert and have a sharp memory according to one Biologist, who spent several years in Nepal using elephants to track Rhinos. "this can be a blessing when you're traveling through tall grass, "he says, "if you drop some items, chances are that you elephant will certainly find it.

"Once an elephant topped dead in its tracks and refused to budge even after the mahout started kicking the animal. The elephant then stepped backwards and picked up a note book in which he had noted down some important things filed notebook, which he had inadvertently dropped.

The mahouts tried to dissuade the animals with one or two half-hearted bangs on their heads with the ankles, but these only produced foolish gurgles from somewhere up at the tops of their trunks. They knew exactly how far they could go.

Elephants in Zoos

It is estimated that there are about 1,200 elephants in zoos, half in Europe. And Female elephants make up 80 percent of the zoo population. The media reported. Elephants are often chosen the most popular zoo animals in surveys, and a newborn calf draws hordes of visitors.

Zoo elephants tend to die younger, are more prone to aggression and are less capable of breeding compared with the hundreds of thousands of elephants left in the wild. *Many zoo elephants, though hardy, spend too much time cramped indoors, get little exercise and become susceptible to infections and arthritis from walking on concrete floors.*

Elephants have a hard time being cooped up in zoos. *They suffer from arthritis, foot problems and premature death. Elephants in some zoos are tethered (a tether is a rope or a chain which is used to tie an animal to a post/ or to a tree, so that the animal will have only a very limited space to move around.* They have also been observed sadistically torturing ducks and crushing them with their feet. Many zoos have come to conclusion that zoos cannot meet the needs of elephants and have made a decision not keep them anymore - I personally welcome their decision.

Attention was drawn to the issue after the deaths of four elephants in less than a year in 2004 and 2005 at two U.S. zoos. Two of three African elephants housed at Chicago's Lincoln Park Zoo died over four months. Animal rights activists charged their deaths were hastened by the stress brought on by the elephants' 2003 move from San Diego.

35 elephants died from a rare lung infection and Peaches, at 55 the oldest of some 300 elephants in U.S. captivity, suffered from organ failure. When two elephants in San Francisco's zoo died within weeks of each other, the resulting outcry prompted the zoo to close its exhibit and opt to send its remaining elephants to a California sanctuary against the wishes of the American Zoo and Aquarium Association.

After the controversy, several zoos---including ones in Detroit, Philadelphia, Chicago, San Francisco and the Bronx---decided to phase out their elephant exhibits, citing insufficient funds and lack of space to adequately care for the animals. Some elephants were sent to a 2,700 sanctuary in other States.

But critics say captivity is both physically and mentally stressful. "In the old days, when you didn't have television, children would see animals for the first time at the zoo and it had an educational component," an animal behaviorist said. "Now the zoos claim they're preserving the disappearing species, preserving embryos and genetic material. But you don't need to do that in a zoo.

Calves born in captivity have higher mortality rates and survivors often have to be isolated for a time from their inexperienced mothers, who may trample them. Based on the Oxford University report that found 40 percent of zoo elephants engage in stereo typical behavior, the report's sponsor, Britain's Royal Society for the Prevention of Cruelty to Animals, urged European zoos to stop importing and breeding elephants and to phase out exhibits.

Zoo elephants reportedly prefer women keepers. They sometimes also masturbate a lot. Describing one female elephant, a zoo keeper told the media. "Every time you'd turn around, there she'd be, getting off on a log."

Based on the Oxford University report that found 40 percent of zoo elephants engage in stereo- typical behavior, the report's sponsor, Britain's Royal Society for the Prevention of Cruelty to Animals, urged European zoos to stop importing and stop breeding elephants and to phase out exhibits.

Elephants in Circus

Elephants that work in circuses are trained to kick balls, balanced balls, roller skate, dance, perform tricks, place wreaths around people's necks, stand on their hind legs. Elephants in Kenya have been observed turning on a faucet and captive elephants have been known to unscrew the bolts on their cages.

But the animal performers are often subjected to physical and mental torture.

A young elephant calf tied up with rope, his mother nowhere in sight, while a group of "trainers" contort the young animal into the positions he needs to learn to perform.

Sometimes the training can turn deadly. In 2004, an 8-month-old calf after he fell off a platform during training and broke two legs. A few years earlier, a 3-year-old drowned after running into the water to escape from his trainer's bull hook.

Baby circus elephants around the world go through a similar process to prepare them for performances and make them docile enough to handle. The training process is painful, both physically and psychologically - the baby elephants are often brutally ripped away from their mothers before training begins.

Anyway, we can be very happy that the world community has realised the use any animals in various human entertaining activities, like, trekking, circus, Zoo and display of animals other private /public ceremonies are already banned in many countries and will be banned soon in other countries also very soon. and the be in in any ha can very soon.

13
Save Elephant

Let us have a look at the major threat that elephants/animals facing today.

Threat to Elephants

Poaching: The most severe threat facing African elephants is poaching and the now illegal global ivory trade. More than 100 elephants are killed every day for their tusks. In recent years, poaching of elephants has increased exponentially, even in the face of global outrage and treaties, leading to dramatic reductions in this already vulnerable species. Asian elephants are being targeted by poachers for their skin which is used for commercial and medicinal purposes.

Habitat Loss: Habitat loss fuels a vicious cycle in the elephant ecosystem. Rising and expanding human populations reduce the habitat available to elephants, putting them in closer proximity to humans, leading to more elephant killings.

Climate Change: Elephants are already feeling the impacts of global warming. Droughts lead to food shortages and reduced habitat. Droughts also disrupt the mating season, which leads to fewer offspring.

You Can Save Elephants by:

Joining the Movement to Stop the Ivory Trade: While international trade in ivory is banned, illegal trade continues to thrive and ivory poaching has more than doubled since 2007. Many countries like the U.S. and China have enacted a near-total ban on ivory in order to stop the flow of ivory trade within their countries borders. borders. Additionally, individual states in the U.S. are taking local action passing laws that ban the import, sale, purchase, or possession of ivory. Find out if your state or country is fighting to protect elephants and check out.

Protect Elephants from Entertainment: Elephants are used for a variety of human entertainment – from circuses to elephant-back rides – which contribute to their endangerment. It is important to speak out against these cruel practices. In the U.S., seven states and 149 other localities have passed legislation to address the cruel treatment of circus animals or to ban animal acts entirely. Find out if circus animals are banned where you live. If not, contact your elected leaders asking them to ban the use of wild or exotic animals in circuses.

Practice Sustainable Tourism: Only travel with companies that are certified as sustainable. If you are fortunate enough to see an **animal in the wild, make sure that your interaction is respectful.**

Contributing to the Foundations: There are many foundations and voluntary organisations across the world working on Save Elephant and Save Elephant Movement projects across the world.

In addition to this, as a citizen of your country, country, each one of us has the moral responsibility to ensure that all type of animals whether domestic / or wild animals are not ill-treated, no cruelty to the animals and protect them, especially we must be more concerned about the 'threatened / endangered' species like elephants. You must also report any animal abuse/ cruelty to any animals in your knowledge and report he matter to the authorities concerned.

Old Age Home for Aged Elephants
An initiative by Kerala Forest Dept.

A part of Save Elephant Movement

An innovative Project under planning under the Kerala Govt. The Kerala Forest Department is coming up with an innovative idea of an Old Age Home for the elephants suffering from age. Not only that, a nursery for baby elephants is also in the offing.

The Elephant Rehabilitation Centre getting set up at Kottur in Thiruvananthapuram district, will provide facilities for caring of the aged elephants as well as baby elephants often rescued from the wild.

Tenders have already been invited for the Phase I work of the Rehabilitation Centre. The Rs. 105 crores project aims at creating a space where elephants can dwell peacefully in a natural environment.

The Old Age home for Elephants will provide care for those elephants, weakened due to ther old age. And the Nursery will have facilities to care for Baby elephants rescued from the wild under various circumstances.

This is a very inovaive idea This Old age Home will be of great help to the aged elephant kept in captive and furer used them as working animals, will certainly make them physically very weak some of them become so weak that they may not be able to eat their food or drink water. in such cases, generally sr whci reduces their life span very considerably.

Gnerally, such old and weak elephants are put to sleep and take away their valuable Tusk, sell it off for a high value and make lot fo money. Who else can serve his master/ owner, even after their death, with their lifeless body?

© WildTrails of India

CPSIA information can be obtained
at www.ICGtesting.com
Printed in the USA
LVRC020742140520
655544LV00011B/205